Spiritual Encounters And Other Strange Stories From The Little Red School-House

Carsten R. Jorgensen

and

Dana Woodard

Copyright © 2018 Carsten R Jorgensen And Dana Woodard

All rights reserved.

No part of this book may be reproduced, stored in a database or other retrieval system, or transmitted in any form, by any means now existing or later discovered, including without limitation mechanical, electronic, photographic or otherwise, without the express prior written permission of the publisher.

Written and published in Canada.

ISBN-13: 978-0-9938776-3-6

CONTENTS

1	Introduction (by Carsten R.)	1
2	Katrine Bundtmager	9
3	Sine Bundtmager	11
4	Niels Peter Dam	17
5	Viggo	21
6	Vera	25
7	Gerda And The Ghost	31
8	Carsten	35
9	Richard & Doris Jorgensen	39
10	Thibeault Hill	41
11	Heather	47
12	Chisholm	55
13	Grahamvale Road	67
14	Oakwood	79
15	Riley	85
16	Lake Heights	87
17	Little Red School-House	91
18	Strange Lights	109
19	Message From A Genie	117

1. INTRODUCTION

"If one door closes and another one opens, your house is probably haunted" - unknown

The people of our time are very worldly oriented. They pride themselves in not being superstitious. However, we are often hearing about the supernatural. People consider the stories to be mostly flights of fancy; that is, unless they experience it themselves.

I have talked with some atheists who believe that there is nothing in the world except the physical. To these people, the supernatural is caused by overactive imaginations, hallucinations, or some type of psychosis.

When talking to religious people, I find that there is a belief in the supernatural. These people attribute the supernatural to either, angels, demons, or God Himself. Examples are the appearance of the Virgin Mary, or the appearance of Jesus Christ. I have heard of one person in the early 1900's who claimed that he was playing cards with a group of people in a pub for money. The person dropped a card and bent under the table to pick it up. There he saw that the card player who was constantly winning had feet with cloven hooves.

The following is a description of only some of the types of creatures often found in supernatural encounters:

ELVES

Elves have been found throughout history. There are two types of elves who are very different from each other. There are small elves and tall elves. When describing the small elves, the term "elf" here is incorrect. The English call them elves which is confusing considering the other type of elves are tall elves. The small elves are known by different names in other European countries. In Sweden and Norway they are known as "Tomte". Germans call them "Erdmanleins" or "Heinzemannchens". In many parts of the world they are known as "Gnomes". In Denmark they are called Nisser. The singular is "Nisse" (pronounced "Nissah").

The most distinctive things about Nisser are their red pointed hats and their love of looking after animals. Reports of the Nisser are found way back in pre-history. They were little folk who lived in forests and inside cliffs and hills. They interacted with people on occasion; sometimes in a friendly way and sometimes not. When people started to build houses, the Nisser found that it was more comfortable to live in the houses than in the hills. Therefore, they moved into the people's houses and took up residence there.

The Nisser living in the homes of people would bring the people good luck and would sometimes do wonderful things for their human families there. The Nisser loved a clean house. One thing which pleased the Nisser was to keep the house clean, neat and tidy. All they asked for in return was a bowl of porridge and a glass of glogg each night. However if a Nisse was mistreated by a human, the Nisser would become very mischievous (but never malevolent).

There was a story of a Nisse who became so mischievous, that the farmer who owned the house decided to move away from this Nisse and bought another house. On moving day he loaded his wagon with all his belongings, hitched his horse to the wagon and away he went. When he was halfway to his new house, he heard a rustling behind him in the wagon. He turned and saw the Nisse pop up from his pile of belongings. The Nisse looked at him and said, "So we are moving today!".

In Ireland, Nisser are called "Leprechauns". There people used to go into the forest to attempt to capture a leprechaun because they believed that leprechauns had much gold stored in their burrows.

The people of the twentieth century decided to have the little elves removed from their homes. They arranged for the little elves to be rounded up and sent far away. These elves were transported to a concentration camp at the north pole where they were forced to labour in a work shop making toys. However some of the little elves escaped and found their way into modern homes.

Jule Nisser - by Jenny Nyström

When it was time to round up the little elves, the people of Denmark hid their little elves because they loved them. Therefore the little Nisser escaped capture and continue to live happily in Denmark. There at Christmas time they dress in red and they are called "Jule Nisser". Sometimes a little Nisse will make a little Christmas present for a member of his host family. The lady of the house makes a special porridge or pudding for the Nisser at Christmas time.

THE REAL ELVES

The other type of elves are tall and handsome. They look a lot like the elves portrayed in the movies: "The Hobbit" and "The Lord of the Rings". In Denmark they came out in the mist. During the pre-Viking age, the Viking age, and during the middle ages the people did not go far from their home when there was a mist. Some people who ventured into the forest in a mist were captured by the elves and taken to the palace of the elven king. There they were treated extremely well. They were treated to lavish feasts and there was lots of music, dancing and parties.

After a few days these guests of the elven king traveled home to discover that during their stay with the elves more than a hundred years had gone by.

Strangers owned their homes. Everybody they used to know were dead and buried.

GHOSTS

Ghosts are believed to be the spirits (souls) of people who have died. There are places in the world where they say that spirits of the dead are present: haunted houses, haunted castles, haunted graveyards, haunted hills and moors. Many people avoid such places. Even people who pride themselves in not being superstitious avoid some haunted places. Under special conditions ghosts have appeared to people. Such conditions include just before someone dies and just after someone has died.

The words 'supernatural' and 'unnatural' belong in a different category. Everything in this world is natural. We use the term 'nature' to indicate what is away from the man-made civilization. Instead of the term 'supernatural' I prefer the term 'spiritual'.

I believe that every family has stories of spiritual encounters. The stories in this book are all taken from true life experiences of my family. All the following stories here have actually happened.

2. KATRINE BUNDTMAGER

Katrine as told to her sister Nielsine

Katrine worked as a live-in nanny and house keeper for a machinist who was married to a woman who was very sick with Multiple Sclerosis. Katrine and the man fell in love but since he was already married their affair was kept very secret because divorce was almost unheard of back in those days.

From this affair Katrine became pregnant and had a daughter. When she found out she was pregnant she went back home to live with her parents. She did not tell anyone who the father was, not even her parents, and no one guessed that it was the man that she worked for.

A year or two later Katrine went back to work for the same man. Once again she became pregnant and once again she went back home to her parents to have the child. This time she had a son. Still no one knew who the father was and she refused to tell. She wanted to marry the man but it never came to pass. She remained single for the rest of her life.

After her children had grown up, married and moved away she eventually ended up taking care of her parents in their old age. At that time there were no electric lights, only lamps. Every night Katrine would be very tired from looking after her parents all day and working on the farm and she would go to bed and sleep soundly without waking until morning. Every night, that is, except one.

On this particular night, she awoke with a very strong feeling that the father of her two children was in the room with her. After getting up and lighting her lamp, she checked the whole house and found no one. She went outside and searched for signs of a vehicle or a bicycle, but again there was no one.

Eventually she went back to bed but she still couldn't shake the feeling that he had been there. The next morning she read in the newspaper that the father of her children had died.

3. SINE BUNDTMAGER

Sine as a teenager

Sine as told to her daughter Vera

When Nielsine (Sine for short) Bundtmager was a teenager, her uncle Carsten came back home to Denmark from the U.S.A. He stayed all winter. The reason he came home was to tell his family that he had become a Christian.

When he did there was a big awakening in his former home town. His brother, Mads Bundtmager, and his wife, along with about a hundred others became committed Christians. Mads even built a big hall as an addition to his house where everyone could get together for their church meetings.

Sine went to those meetings because it was in her home and all of her family was there, but she wasn't really a true believer.

Most of the time Sine was working about 7 kilometers away, so she had to travel home by bicycle to get to the church meetings.

One day Sine showed up wearing a fancy new hat that she had just bought. It was really fancy with lots of artificial flowers and a great big coloured feather sticking up in the back. An elderly lady at the meeting said to her " Sine, you shouldn't decorate yourself like that. Be natural. The Lord doesn't like all that fancy stuff on people." To which Sine replied " If the Lord doesn't like it then he can rip it off."

After the church service Sine got on her bike and started travelling the 7 kilometers back to her place of work. As she travelled a thunderstorm came up with heavy winds and rain. She got to her room where she was staying ok but when she took her hat off, the feather was gone.

She said to herself several times, "He took it off! He really took it off! The Lord took the feather off my hat!" She said that was the day she really began to believe in God.

An Infant Death

Sine as an adult

Carsten as told to him by his mother Vera

My mother had three sisters who were older than her. She also had two brothers, one older than herself and one younger. But she told me that at one time she also had fourth baby sister. My mother's mother, Sine Dam, had kidney poisoning while carrying her so this baby sister, Nancy, was not well. Nancy was born with a water tumour on the back of her head.

On the morning that Nancy was born, Sine heard something heavy fall to the floor. Nobody else had heard the sound. She looked at the place where the sound had come from and could not find anything that had fallen down. She spent all day dropping things on the floor in an effort to try to reproduce the sound that she had heard, but she was unable to do so.

Baby Nancy died during the night. The next day they prepared to bring the infant to the hospital. Her husband, Niels Dam, opened the closet door and got his coat from a coat hanger. As he did, he accidentally knocked a weight from the shelf that they used to hold down scarves or hats. The sound it made was the exact noise which Sine had heard the day before.

THREE CARS

My mother was a little girl and there were not very many cars in the world. Her family used a horse and buggy as did all their neighbours. One evening, her mother stood up and said, "A car just drove up to the house." She went to the door and looked outside. But there was no car.

About an hour later she heard a car and saw the headlights approaching. She announced, "The car stopped outside." She went to the door but there was no car outside.

After about another hour, my grandmother once again said she heard a car approach and that she saw it park just outside. But when she opened the door to see what was going on there was no car. Nobody else had heard nor seen the cars approach.

    In the evening the next day one of my mother's sisters became very ill. It was so bad that they sent for an ambulance which came and took the sick girl to the hospital. Then about an hour after the ambulance had left, another of my mother's sisters was suddenly very sick and an ambulance came and took her to the hospital. After the ambulance had left my mother's remaining sister also became very ill. Again, an ambulance brought the sick girl to the hospital. All three ambulances arrived about an hour apart. The next day they learned that the three girls were suffering from Scarlet Fever.

4. NIELS PETER DAM

Niels Peter Dam (left) and wife Marie (right)

Niels Peter Dam as told to his grand daughter Vera

Niels Peter Dam was a deep-sea commercial fisherman who lived in a little house in Denmark at the top of a big hill. There were no roads, only a path down the hill to the Fjord. Near the base of the hill lived his cousin, Johannes Balle, the only neighbour for miles around, who often went fishing with him. They had a little row-boat tied up in the Fjord and would row out to the larger ship because the ship was too big to come in so close to shore.

One October day Niels went out fishing in the North Sea by himself. At the end of the day a storm came up. As he left the bigger boat and tried to make his way home in the row-boat, the waves grew bigger and bigger and lashed against the row-boat. Soon night fell and it became so dark and foggy that he could no longer see where he was or where he was going.

Just when he thought it couldn't get any worse, one of his oars broke. This left him with no way to steer and since trying to steer with just one oar would just result in him going around in circles.

So he just drifted for awhile with the rain beating down on him and the waves tossing him around until finally he could feel the bottom of the row-boat hit the sandy bottom. He jumped out of the row-boat and into the freezing cold October water of the Fjord and pulled the boat to shore.

His first instinct was to just lie down and go to sleep because he was so tired and so cold from rowing against the waves in the rain, but he knew that if he did then he would freeze to death. So he started walking even though he couldn't see where he was walking to because he had drifted a long way. It was still very dark and stormy and this was before the time of electric lights.

He had hardly any energy left and didn't know if he would ever make it home and thought that he might die out there in the elements. He was about to give up when all of a sudden he felt a firm strong hand on his shoulder and it guided him in a specific direction. He couldn't see or hear anything through the wind and the rain but he thought that his cousin must have seen him struggling in the row-boat and had come to help him. With all the noise from the wind and the waves he knew it was impossible to carry on a conversation so he didn't try to talk.

Eventually he began to recognize where he was. They were going up the path on the hill towards his house. When, at long last, he finally got to his doorway and saw the candle that his wife always kept lit for him, he turned to thank Johannes for his help but no one was there.

The next day he went down to his cousin's house to thank him for his help but Johannes told him that he was not the one who helped him. He had been sleeping and did not even know that Niels was in trouble.

"So now I am convinced it was an angel" says Niels.

Niels Peter Dam walking down the path from his house

5. VIGGO

Old newspaper clipping : "Fisherman Viggo Brejner Kristensen, Taebring, with catcher, and family boat around 1912. He emigrated later to America."

Viggo as told to Vera by her cousin Beryl

At the age of 19 Viggo left Denmark and moved to Chicago, USA. There he married and had children, including a daughter named Beryl. Although he was a commercial fisherman by trade it was during the Great Depression era so he took on jobs wherever he could find them.

Viggo and a friend decided to start a business together and they began picking up ashes from town and hauling them to the local dump in the truck that they had bought together. And so it seemed that things were going OK for a time.

One day back in Denmark, Neilsine (Viggos' sister) had a dream. She dreamt that a vehicle had hit Viggo and that he had been injured badly with a hole in his stomach.

Everyone told her that it was just a dream; that it meant nothing and to just forget about it. But she felt that it was too realistic and it bothered her a great deal. She just knew that something was wrong. Now back then you couldn't just pick up the phone and call and mail was much slower than it is today. A month or so later the family got a letter from Viggo's wife telling them that he was dead.

Apparently while hauling ashes one day, he got out of the truck and went behind it to guide his partner as he was backing up. When Viggo signalled for him to stop, instead of hitting the brakes, his partner stepped on the gas and the truck slammed into Viggo's stomach and crushed him between the truck and a cement wall.

The family believed that it was no accident but were never able to prove it. It was known that Viggo and his partner had a deal that if one of them should die then the other would get the truck and the business. A few days before the incident Viggo had mentioned to his partner that he wanted out of the business to pursue his real trade of commercial fishing. Viggo told his partner that he would sell him his half of the business and the truck. Since this was in the middle of the Great Depression, his partner could not afford to buy Viggo out, so they suspect he had found a way to get everything for free. Since none of this could be proven, the partner ended up with everything and Viggo's death had been labeled as an "accident".

Now Viggo did not die right away. He was taken to the hospital where the doctors tried to save him. But the wound in his stomach got gangrene and there was nothing they could do for him. So he lay in the hospital just waiting to die and his daughter Beryl, who was 19 at the time, sat with him by his side, day and night.

To preserve energy in the Great Depression, most of the hospital was always dark where the light wasn't the most needed. Since Viggo was just waiting to die, there wasn't a great need for light in his room so it was always dark. One evening, the room got intensely bright all of a sudden with a light that was almost blinding. Thinking that perhaps there was a chemical fire or something, Beryl ran out of the room to quickly find a nurse.

When she returned with the nurse the room was dark again. From the darkness Viggo said " Did you see him?" Beryl asked "Who?" To which Viggo replied "Didn't you see Jesus? Jesus was just here! He said that I was to go home with him, but not until Tuesday".

And sure enough, on Tuesday Viggo died. That made a believer out of Beryl.

6. VERA

HELL'S GATE

The tribulations of St. Anthony – by Martin Schongauer

Carsten R. as told to him by his mother, Vera

My mother was born in 1918. She lived with her parents, sisters, and brothers on a small farm on the Island of Mors in the Lim Fjord in Denmark. My mother told me that in the 1920's a young man lived on a small farm nearby. He loved to ride his horse into town, go to a bar and get drunk.

One night the young man had a dream. In his

dream he rode into town, went to the bar, got drunk and began to ride home. He rode past a red brick wall in town. Except he did not make it past the wall. When he reached the middle of the wall, a doorway opened up in the wall. Demons rushed out of the wall. They grabbed the young man and pulled him through the opening of the wall.

The young man shook off the nightmare. That night he rode into the town tavern and got drunk. He then rode home and went to bed. There he had the very same dream. The next night he had the same nightmare. Night after night the wall opened up like a gateway and a flock of demons pulled him through the opening to Hades.

Eventually the dreams bothered the man so much that he began to tell everyone he knew about his nightmares. He went to the wall and examined it. He looked at it and felt it until he was satisfied that no doorway existed there. People in the street who wondered what the young man was doing asked him about it. He explained his dream to them and showed them the exact location of the doorway from where the demons burst out to grab him.

The nightmares persisted. One night the young man rode to town. He went to the tavern. He got drunk. Then when the tavern was closing, he mounted his horse. As he was riding by the brick wall, his horse threw him. He hit the wall and broke his neck which killed him. The part of the wall where he landed was the exact location where the doorway had opened for the demons.

RED MEASLES

Vera and her brother Robert

Vera as told to her granddaughter Dana

In 1927 , when Vera was 9 years old, she became very sick with the Red Measles. Her mother had her in bed with the window blinds closed in order to protect her eyes. She gave her aspirin and took her temperature and tried to make her feel as comfortable as possible.

But it was July, and they had a turnip field that needed tending so her mother tucked her in and said "We will all be out in the field hoeing the turnips. But you go to sleep and we will be back in a couple of hours." And so they left and Vera was alone in the house and she tried to go to sleep.

After some time had gone by Vera began to feel something wet on her face. She put her hand to her face and found that it was wet and sticky with blood. She tried to get out of bed to call her mom but after going a short distance she became so dizzy that she could not stand up. She managed to crawl her way back into bed but by now her pillow and sheets were red and soaked with blood. She realized that the blood was coming from her nose and remembers thinking her mother would be angry with her for messing up the bed.

She began to worry and didn't know what to do until she remembered her mother saying "If you are in trouble, pray to the Lord and he will help you". So she folded her hands and began to pray. "Dear Lord will you send my mom home?".

Moments later the door opened and her mom stood in her room. After her mother got the bleeding to stop and got the blood cleaned up she went over and sat on the edge of Vera's bed and asked "Vera, did you pray to God?" Vera answered "Yes" and then fell asleep.

Later her mother told her that she was in the middle of a row of turnips when she suddenly knew that she had to go home. Her father had said to her mother "Why don't you wait and finish the row?" But her mother said that the feeling was so great that she didn't wait, and she didn't walk. She ran all the way home.

7. GERDA AND THE GHOST

Left to Right: Vera, Gerda, Marietta, Martine

Vera as told to her granddaughter Dana

My mom just had a knee operation in both knees. So she had these white bandages wrapped around her knees and legs. Every night before bed she would change the bandages and back then women only wore skirts, not pants, so they were quite visible.

We lived two houses away from the Lutheran church. The house between our house and the church was the minister's house. Once a month the Lutheran church would have a youth meeting in the evening and all the youth that attended would arrive on their bikes and store them in the stable. My sister

Marietta had gone to one of these meetings earlier in the evening and now it was starting to get dark.

So Gerda, the funny one of my sisters, said to my mom "Why don't we go over to the church and the minister's house right beside and see when they come out if Marietta is with her boyfriend and see how they behave? We can stand in the dark by the minister's house and watch from the dark while they go to get their bicycles."

My mom said "No, I can't do that I have these bandages on my legs. That would be embarrassing. " But Gerda said "Well, they can't see you, it's dark out there. No one will even know you are there. " (Back in those days no one had flash lights).

So Gerda talked her into it and they walked up to the house by the church and waited, knowing that at 11 o'clock all the young people would come spilling out of the church and head for the stable to get their bikes. Gerda and my mother stood with their back up against a short stone wall that lined the near by grave yard.

At the appointed time, suddenly the door opened and everyone came spilling out laughing and chattering happily. There must have been about 50 of them or more.

Unbeknownst to Gerda and her mother, the

church had recently put in electric lights at the stables where there had never been any before. So it was quite a surprise to them when someone switched on the light and there they were standing in plain view.

Gerda with her fast thinking made a loud yelping sound and quickly dove over the stone wall and into the cemetary, leaving her mother standing there all alone. Her mother didn't know what to do. She froze and just stood there hoping that they wouldn't notice her or would think she was just a part of the fixtures and not a person at all.

Where once all the young people were previously chattering happily and were talking loudly, there now was utter silence and they stared in her direction. After a moment or two she finally turned and as quickly as she could, considering she couldn't move so fast after just having surgery, went back home. She was a bit upset with Gerda for leaving her all alone like that, and they never did get a chance to spy on Marietta. But it was soon forgotten and they went to bed quickly before Marietta came home and told them off for spying.

The next morning, before Vera headed off to school her mother said "If anyone talks about last night, pretend that you don't know anything. Don't mention my name or anything. Pretend I was never there." So Vera agreed and headed off to school.

Now most of the kids that Vera went to school with had older brothers and sisters that had attended the youth meeting the night before and they had all heard the story already. It was all anyone could talk about for most of the day. But the story was not what Vera had expected to hear. Instead the kids were saying "There were ghosts in the cemetary last night! My brother told me he saw them." and another would say "Yes, my sister told me that too!"

Since Vera had promised not to tell about her mother and sister being there she pretended not to know about it and instead said "Oh, what happened?"

"There were two ghosts" they said " and when the lights came on the one ghost let out a big whine, jumped over the fence and right back into his grave! The other one was all wrapped up in his burial cloths and he just stood there and everyone was afraid to go near him!"

Even Vera's mother heard about the story from some of the other adults in the community who told her "You may not believe in ghosts but they were there. There were two of them!"

It was a very long time before the town stopped talking about the two ghosts in the cemetery. Vera, Gerda and their mother never did tell anyone in town that the two ghosts were actually them.

8. CARSTEN

GEORGE'S DOG

Carsten R as experienced in 1954

In 1954 my parents bought a hundred acre farm near Campbellford, Ontario. I was twelve years old. We lived on top of a huge hill. Our lane way was about half a mile long. On one side of the hill the road went towards school and Campbellford. On the other side lived a newly wed couple. The young man was George.

George got a job cutting timber on a wood lot. In the morning he put his chain saw in his half ton truck and drove over our big hill and continued to the wood lot where he spent the day felling trees. This was his routine every day.

One day George's collie dog followed George's half ton truck. When George went over the hill, the dog stayed at the bottom of the hill. There the dog sat down, raised his head and howled. He howled and howled. We could hear him howl all day. Towards the end of the day the dog stopped howling. At that time we also got the news from a neighbour that George had died.

George had been felling trees on a hill. One of the trees he cut down fell up slope on the hill. When the tree hit the ground, the branches made the tree bounce. The tree bounced back at George and the trunk took out his chest. The dog had howled because he had the premonition that this was about to happen.

PHOTOGRAPHY

Carsten R. as experienced in 1962

In 1962, I started my studies at Queen's University in Kingston Ontario which led to my Honours BSc in Biology. While there I spent three years working for the geneticist, Hans Stich. One of his graduate students was Madan Joneja, a student from India. Madan was a photographer. He photographed chromosomes, biological tissues and cells. He also photographed people. There was a dark room in the university where Madan developed his pictures and sometimes I did the development for him.

Madan had also been to a couple of funerals where he took pictures. On many of the pictures, there among the mourners, was also found the dead person. No, not the corpse, but the person himself who seemed as alive as the living. The only noticeable difference was that the dead person appeared a little more pale than the other mourners.

Dr. Stich would have a gathering, once a month, at his home in the evening with his graduate students and me. Sometimes he would invite other professors and their graduate students too. On one occasion Hans Stich invited a Minister. Madan brought his funeral pictures and there was a discussion of ghosts.

The discussion centered along the line of scientific studies of ghosts. The usual topics of studies of cold spots and other endeavours of ghost hunters was brought up with no satisfactory conclusions. There was mention of a couple of attempts made by biologists to explain the phenomenon which had produced no results. Instead of conclusions there was only awe and entertainment. At the end Hans Stich stated that the ghosts were intelligent beings and were not going to let themselves be examined in any scientific experiment.

9. RICHARD & DORIS JORGENSEN

Richard Jorgensen

Carsten R. as experienced in 1966

In 1966 I graduated from Queen's University. I did not attend my graduation. Instead I travelled with my parents and brother Willy to Denmark for a visit. We went by Scandinavian Airlines flying from Ottawa to Kastrup. My father's brother, Richard, picked us up at the airport and took us to his home.

When we reached my Uncle's home there was a great feast of open faced sandwiches and a beer at each setting. Richard's wife was Doris. His two little girls approximately aged nine and ten were Pia and Iben. Richard had two sons who were grown and had their own homes.

My uncle Richard was an architect. He told us that he had been working in Greenland and Doris and the girls had moved over there to be with him during the project. When the work was complete, Richard obtained tickets for Denmark on a ship. Then they celebrated and prepared to depart the next day.

During the night my uncle dreamed that it was the next day. The family travelled down to the dock and boarded the ship. In the dream when the ship was halfway between Greenland and Denmark it sank. Richard, Doris and the girls all drowned.

When the morning came the family prepared to travel. On the way to the dock Richard told Doris about his dream. Doris was shocked because she had dreamed the same dream. The dreams were identical. When they reached the dock, they considered that the dreams were too real and decided to not get on the ship. They all went back to where they had been living.

Sure enough, just as the dreams had predicted, halfway between Greenland and Denmark the ship that they were supposed to be on sank.

10. THIBEAULT HILL

Carsten R. as experienced in 1969

In 1968, I fell head over heels in love with a Game Warden's daughter, Brenda Black. In 1969 we became engaged to be married. We bought a small house on top of Thibeault Hill just outside of North Bay Ontario. On top of the hill, going north, there was a convenience store. From there a small county road that went west. A little ways down the road were two houses. We bought the second one. It was a red brick house with an attached garage. The house was one storey with a basement. In the kitchen was the stairs leading into the basement and in the basement was a green door leading into the garage.

    Brenda was working for a family in Birch Haven and she resided with them. I moved out of my apartment and into our new house. The house had two bedrooms and was very cozy. Sometimes when I went into the bathroom, I would hear voices. They were the voices of people talking. The conversations were not loud enough that I could make out the words. When Brenda was over to visit, she suggested that the voices might be echoes picked up from somebody's radio which would send echoes off the walls of the bathroom. I thought this was an adequate explanation.

    When Brenda had left and I was alone again and went to the bathroom, the voices were there again. I went outside to check for radios. There were no cars outside and mine was sitting quietly in the garage. There was only one house nearby and it was quiet. I concluded that it was not a nearby radio that these voices were coming from. How could a radio or radios from farther away produce animated conversations in my bathroom?

    One night, while I was in bed sleeping, I woke up suddenly to the slamming of the basement door. Had someone broke into the house? The door leads into the attached garage so it could not be the wind blowing it shut. I shook myself awake and went down the stairs to the basement. The basement door was not only shut, it was also locked.

The next night the basement door slammed again with a very loud bang. Once again I got up, went down stairs and checked the door. It was locked. Almost every night the slamming of the basement door woke me up. Finally I stopped going down to the basement to check the door. Instead I just rolled over and went back to sleep.

One day Brenda let me know that she had to get up early the next morning for an appointment. She was still living across town in Birch Haven so I promised to give her a wake up call. I have always been good at getting up in the morning. Besides, maybe the basement door would wake me up. However, that particular morning I found myself unable to wake up. I was asleep and conscious of trying to wake up but my body refused to co-operate. I was in a sort of dream state and knew I was asleep. I did not want to let Brenda down so I yelled her name as loud as I could. I yelled her name over and over each time louder than the last. That morning I received a phone call from Brenda. She had heard me yelling and it woke her up.

On April 25, 1970, Brenda and I were married. Then on March 1, 1971 our daughter Dana was born. After Dana learned to walk and talk, we sometimes heard her talking when she was not in the same room as Brenda and me. On occasion I sometimes thought I heard someone talking with her. However it is not unusual for a child to have an imaginary friend.

Dana at the house on Thibeault Hill

One day, when Dana was about 3, she walked away from the house. We got a call by someone saying that Dana had walked to the end of the road and had crossed the highway to the convenience store. We picked her up and took her home. We talked to her about it and she said that her friend had wanted her to come with him to the store. The imaginary friend was becoming too real.

We obtained a Ouija board. We practiced placing our fingertips on the marker and seeing how it would move. We asked simple questions and received simple answers. Then we became serious and asked serious questions. "Who are you?"

This got no answer.

"Are you male or female?"

MALE

"What is your name?"

DIETER

We never did find out who Dieter was, why he was friends with Dana, or what he wanted. We eventually moved away and the house was torn down many years later. Dana has no recollection of Dieter.

11. HEATHER

Carsten and Brenda with their children Anika, Heather, Dana, and Carsten at their home on Trout Lake.

Carsten R. as experienced in 1976

We eventually moved to Peninsula Road on Trout Lake where we transformed a cottage into a permanent home. There was a beautiful lake front with a sand beach and a dock. We now had four children: Dana, Heather, Anika and Carsten.

Rex

One day in 1976 we were on the lawn between the house and the beach. Heather, who was three years old stated, "Farmor's dog died." (Farmor was my mother, Vera. Farmor means "Father's Mother" in Danish). Heather went on to tell us exactly what kind of injuries the dog had.

The next time I talked to my mother on the phone, she was very sad. Her German Shepherd, Rex, had just died. The time of death was the exact time and date when Heather had announced it to us on the lawn and the injuries were exactly as Heather had stated they were.

E.W. Norman, the school that Dana and Heather attended while living in their home on Trout Lake.

Brenda as experienced in 1979

    Heather has always been psychic. She lost a lot of it as she got older. It used to be creepy when she was a tiny child. When ever her dad was thinking about getting a hammer for a wood working project or thinking about being cold and needing a sweater she would go and get it without him having to say a word.

    One day, when Heather was about 6 years old, I was headed into town and in my head I was thinking that if I got back in time I would stop by the school and pick Heather up so we could go do something together. I never mentioned it to her I just thought it to myself. But I was running late and ran out of time so I didn't go to pick her up. But Heather had heard in her head that I was picking her up. So as I was driving home there I found her walking down by Trout Lake. She had left school and was walking along the highway. She was walking home.

Heather's version of the above story as experienced in 1979

When I was in kindergarten mom was going to do some errands and thought to herself "If I have enough time I will pick Heather up after school". She never told me this but I heard her saying it in my head. So I told my bus driver that my mom was picking me. The bus driver thought nothing of it and drove away so I waited for a bit and when mom didn't come I started walking home. Just by chance mom saw me walking as she was driving home and picked me up. Mom was really mad at the teachers and the bus driver for letting me go by myself.

Heather

Heather as as experienced as a child (date not recollected)

One day I was riding in the car with dad and I kept telling him "Drive careful" and "Be careful" over and over again. So dad did drive very carefully but later that day a car backed into our car.

Farfar and Heather

Heather as as experienced September 29, 1985

The night Farfar died (Farfar means "Father's Father" in Danish) he appeared in my room. It was late at night and he just stood there. He didn't say anything but I knew by his presence that he had come to say good-bye. Then about 5 minutes later mom and dad got the phone call telling them that he had died and we all got up and got dressed and made the 6 hour drive to Campbellford. I remember that usually I prayed every night for Farfar and Farmor and that was the first night ever that I had forgotten to pray for him.

Jim Varney

Heather as as experienced February 9, 2000

I also had a dream once that the actor from the movie Ernest Goes To Camp (Jim Varney) had died. He died the very next day.

* Photo of Jim Varney is believed to be 'public domain' from website:
http://diamondbaynhatrang.info/pages/j/jim-varney-movies/

12. CHISHOLM

The house on Village Road in Chisholm

VILLAGE ROAD

In February of 1981 our family bought a piece of property in rural Chisholm township with an unfinished house on it. At the time the roads were all just numbered by concession but today it is known as Village Road. The house was a new build but it was mostly just a frame with the roof and the outer walls erected. We moved in right away and for a long time we all lived together in one room with no running water, no hydro and just a wood stove for heat. The kids slept in bunk beds and our parents had a bed at one side of the room. We would play board games in the evening by the light of a Coleman lantern.

When spring came we opened up the adjoining room and insulated it and made the area that much bigger so that we had a kitchen. We were now living in two rooms. Shortly after that our uncle Harry came to stay with us for a few months. It was a bit crowded but we didn't mind too much. We knew it would only be temporary.

It wasn't until we had lived there for some time before we started experiencing strange things.

THROUGH THE WALL

Carsten A. as experienced in 1982

Our parents had gone out for the evening and something had scared me so I had crawled into bed with my uncle Harry.

As I lay there I saw, emerging from the wall, the white form of a woman. It went over to Anika who was sleeping in another bed in the room. Anika sat upright without waking up and followed this white woman right through the wall.

I don't know how long they were gone for but when they came back through the wall Anika was still asleep. The white woman put her back into bed, however, she put Anika into the wrong bed. She put Anika into my bed; the one I had been sleeping in before I had crawled in with uncle Harry.

When we woke up in the morning Anika was still in my bed where the white woman had left her.

INVISIBLE PREDATOR

Recreation of the rabbit hutch that used to stand outside the bedroom window

Dana as experienced in 1984

Eventually when we started doing renovations in the rest of the house each of my siblings and I got our own room in the upstairs part of the house. My room was the first on the right as you went up the stairs and the window over looked the driveway.

At the top of the driveway we had built a rabbit hutch with metal mesh for a floor. Since we were out in the country and surrounded by forest and wild animals such as fox, wolves, weasels, bears, and other animals that could potentially be predators to the rabbits we had built the hutch up on four legs in a stilt like fashion. From my bed, which was right under the window, looking down on the rabbit hutch I could see the entire ground under the hutch.

Early one morning just as the sun was beginning to rise I was awakened by the sounds of the rabbits stomping their feet on the bottom of their cage as they do when they are scared or nervous. Then I could hear the noise of the scurrying of feet as though something was running around underneath the hutch trying to get at the rabbits.

I quickly sat up and looked out the window to see what animal was after our rabbits. But although I could continue to hear the sound of scurrying feet under the rabbit hutch, there was nothing there. There was no predator to be seen anywhere near the cage at all. I was confused but I didn't want to go outside and wake up everyone in the house for nothing so I just sat there looking and waiting to catch a glimpse of something. After a moment the rabbits settled down and all became quiet again.

SOMETHING AT THE END OF THE BED

Dana as experienced in 1985

I was awakened very early in the morning just before the sun had come up. It wasn't so dark that I couldn't see everything in my room but it was still dark enough that I didn't really want to be awake. I didn't know what had woken me up I was just awake.

As I lay there trying to fall back to sleep, all of a sudden some invisible force picked up the foot of my bed and started shaking it up and down. The foot of my bed raised at least three or four inches off the floor as it was being shaken.

I was scared to death and didn't know what to

do. It stopped after a moment but I was too afraid to get out of bed. At the same time I was too afraid to go back to sleep. So I just lay there huddled in the top corner of my bed under the covers waiting for about an hour for the sun to fully come up. When the sunlight did finally come spilling into my room and I was sure that there was nothing there I got out of there fast. I never mentioned it to anyone until I was much older.

STRANGE NOISE AT THE ROCK

The boulder covered in snow in front of the house

Heather as experienced in 1986

There is a big boulder just within the tree line beside the road not far from the house in Chisholm. We would often go there as kids to sit and talk and watch the cars go by, (what little cars that ever did go by that is. We lived in a rural area where there was hardly any traffic) or to play. One day Anika and I were sitting there when a big loud groaning sound like a "Whoooo!!" sounded out directly behind us. We jumped and turned expecting to see someone standing there, but no one and nothing was there. We never did figure out what it was.

THE SCREAM

Carsten A. as experienced in 1990

I came home from school extremely tired one day so I went to lie down for a while. Despite being tired I couldn't fall asleep so I got up after a while and puttered around the house.

As I walked around the house I felt as though the rest of the family were acting a bit odd. They were acting almost as though I wasn't there or that I was in their way or something. Since I felt like I was just in everyone's way I went back to bed to try again to take a nap.

As I lay there, the wind picked up outside and there was this high whistling noise. At that same moment I felt a hand and arm come up through the mattress and through my chest from under the bed. The hand was on my face holding me down.

In the next instant there was a loud scream in my right ear. I couldn't move; partially from fear and partially from being held down by the hand.

When the scream stopped I couldn't hear out of my right ear for a couple of days afterwards. No one else had heard the scream; only me.

(Note: Dana had switched bedrooms about a year previous to this and her room was now at the other end of the hall. Carsten's room, where this happened, was now Dana's old bedroom . The same room where Dana had her bed shaken a few years before).

DREAM CREATURE

Carsten A. as experienced in 1990

One night I had what I thought was a dream. It involved this weird creature that was about two feet tall with a large head that looked almost like a mini T-Rex but with long ears. It's legs resembled kangaroo legs. In the dream it bit me on my thigh. The whole experience was very dream like but when I woke up there were bite marks on my thigh.

THE FIRE AND THE BLUE LADY

Carsten A. as experienced in 1991

I often felt as though there were more than one entity in the house and that they battled with one another. There was one incident in particular that confirmed that for me.

It was late one winter night when I woke up with bright lights just outside my bedroom door way. When I stepped out into the hallway to investigate, the whole stairwell was on fire. I didn't know what to do; there was nobody else awake.

All of a sudden I saw coming towards me down the hall a blue apparition. It was similar to the white lady I had seen when I was younger. It hovered above the floor and came right up to me. Then it turned towards the fire and started spinning like a whirl wind. It went directly into the fire and sucked all the fire up and continued down the stairs and out through the wall and straight outside.

Thinking that I must have just dreamt this, I went back to bed and went back to sleep. I thought nothing of it when I first woke up. I thought it was just a weird dream. However when I went to the stairwell I could see that, although the stairwell was almost back intact, there were still little burn marks that were slowly disappearing.

I got ready for school and went out to catch the bus. As I waited for the bus I looked down the road and off to the side was a perfectly shaped rectangular patch the size of our stairwell where the snow was melted. I believe that was the spot where the blue lady took the fire.

13. GRAHAMVALE ROAD

The house on Grahamvale Road in Chisholm

When we think of strange goings-on and haunting we usually hear about the deaths of previous owners or some tragedy that has happened. However, in the case of both the Chisholm house on Village Road and the house about ¾ of a kilometer down the road from it on Grahamvale Road there had never been a house erected on these spots prior to the ones that stand now. We can only speculate that perhaps the strange things originate from the land itself and not from the buildings. Since we do not know the history of the land we can not be sure.

"Do you know the cause of Fairy Rings" - cigarette card from the George Arents collection

Interestingly enough though there is a rather large fairy ring growing in the front yard of the house on Grahamvale Road. A fairy ring, is a naturally occurring ring or arc of mushrooms. This particular ring is about 15 feet across. There is plenty of folklore associated with fairy rings; from the belief that fairy rings are the result of elves or fairies dancing to the idea that they are portals to the dwelling place of the fairies.

Sometimes some wisdom can be found in folklore. For example, * "moonshine distillers traditionally discard the first 50ml of distillate known sometimes as the fairy portion. Science tells us that the first few drops from a still contain nasty and unwanted substances like methanol which have a lower boiling point than alcohol and therefore come out of the still first."

* From https://www.facebook.com/Medieval.Ireland

Whether or not there is any connection between the fairy ring and the land, strange occurences are still periodically experienced in the houses that are on this land.

The stairs leading up to the art studio (on the right at the top of the stairs) in the house on Grahamvale Road

Dana as experienced in January 1988

When I was about 16 years old I would sometimes house sit and pet sit for our neighbours down the road while they would go away to Florida. On one of these occasions I had been there for about a day or two and was enjoying the solitude of watching TV in the living room near a cozy fireplace, when all of a sudden the radio in the art studio came on full blast.

I ran up the stairs to the art studio where the noise was coming from to see what was going on and to turn the radio off. I looked around but there was no explanation for why it would have turned on and no one else was in the house.

My sister, Anika, ended up buying that house many years later and my daughter, Riley, and I eventually moved in with her for a short spell sometime after that. Riley and I were living in the downstairs of the house while Anika and Christian lived in the upstairs. Christian was working in Ottawa most of the time and was only ever home on occasional weekends. Strange things were always happening in that house and so I began keeping a journal of all the unusual things that happened.

Back door to the workshop in the house on Grahamvale Rd

October 2003

My dog, Balto was barking at the back workshop door. He was shaking and afraid to go near it. He has never acted that way before nor since. When I opened the door, no one and nothing was there.

October 2003

Riley and I were living in the downstairs of Anika's house. We came home one evening from spending the day in town and no one else was home so the house was dark.

Riley went down stairs and I turned the hall light on, which is the first light switch available when you get in the door, and left the living room light off.

I went down stairs to grab some wood for the fire and when I got back upstairs the living room light was on and the hall light was off. Riley had not come back upstairs and no one else was in the house.

The bathroom on the left and bedroom straight ahead

I went upstairs to take a shower one evening and the door to the room at the end of the hall, just beside the bathroom, was open. When I came out of the bathroom after I was done my shower, the bedroom door was closed.

The only people in the house at the time were myself and Riley; and Riley hadn't been upstairs. There were also no open windows or any sort of breeze that could have closed the door.

November 2003

Anika said that she was in the laundry room and could hear people whispering but couldn't make out what they were saying. I would occasionally hear very faint music in the house when there was no radio, computer or television on.

December 2003

We would often hear a beeping noise for about a month in many different parts of the house. Never in the same place. We thought it might be a cell phone but it wasn't. We thought it could be a fire alarm with a battery that was dying but the fire alarms were all hard-wired into the walls, and that wouldn't have explained why we were hearing it in different places. We thought of all the electronic things that it could be but it was never any of those things. In January it stopped as mysteriously as it had begun.

The kitchen in the house on Grahamvale Road

March 7, 2004 – 3 pm

I was watering the plants in the kitchen. I turned off the faucet and and turned around to put a plant back on top of the fridge a few steps away. I heard water running and turned around to see that the faucet was back on again after I had just turned it off.

March 8, 2004 – 1 a.m.
I came out of the bathroom and turned off the light. I leaned into the next room which was Anika's office to talk to her while she was on the computer. When I turned a moment later the bathroom light was back on again.

March 9, 2004 – 4 a.m.
I was just about to close my eyes to say a prayer when I saw a black shadow zip past, very fast, in my bedroom.

March 25, 2004 – 7pm
I went downstairs to get some chicken out of the freezer. I noticed that the light was on in the adjoining room but I figured that I would leave it on because my hands were full and I planned to go back down stairs in a few minutes anyways.

I put supper in the oven and then went back down stairs to find that the light was already off. Riley had been engrossed in her N64 game of Banjo Tooie all day and she was the only one else in the house. I didn't think it was her but I asked her anyways. "Did you go downstairs at all?" She said that she had not.

April 1, 2004 – 6:23 a.m.
I was lying on my bed downstairs with the dog sleeping on one side of me and my cat sleeping on the top of me. I felt the bed move as though a small animal such as another cat had jumped up near my

head. My cat lifted her head and looked in that direction as though she had noticed it too. But there was nothing there.

April 1, 2004 – 6:53 a.m.

My cat had moved down to sleep at my feet by this time and my dog was still asleep. I felt the "invisible cat" step on my leg as it went from one side of the bed to the other. There was nothing there and there was no indication that my cat had noticed anything this time.

The living room in the house on Grahamvale Road

April 8, 2004 – 1:45 a.m.

I was standing by the fireplace in the living room looking aimlessly at the window as I went over a discussion in my head I had that evening with some friends about a game that we had been playing.

I noticed in the reflection in the window a white cat that slinked by and disappeared under the coffee table. I thought it was my sister's cat, Wookie, at first and wondered why her reflection looked so white. But when I looked under the table and all around there was no cat.

Wookie was curled up, asleep, on the stairs and my cat, Sanders, was downstairs sleeping. I think I may have seen the "invisible cat" from my bed a few days earlier.

BATHROOM WARNING

The bathroom in the house on Grahamvale Road

April 15, 2004 – 4 pm

Anika was outside raking leaves and Riley and her cousin Kendra were outside playing ball. I was the only one in the house.

I went to the bathroom to plug my curling iron in so that I could curl my hair. As I was reaching for it in the bottom cupboard I heard in a loud, raspy whisper that seemed to come from over near the shower "Stay away from there!" I plugged my curling iron in and left the room quickly.

April 21, 2004 – 8 am

I thought I heard Anika moving about upstairs and I wanted to talk to her about something, so I stood in my doorway for a minute listening to see if she was awake yet.

As I stood there a large animal went past my feet

from my left to my right in front of me. I thought it was my dog, Balto, at first until I turned around and saw Balto sitting there right behind me.

So I figured that maybe I was mistaken about the size of the animal and maybe it was really my cat. But a quick scan of my room indicated otherwise. Sanders was sitting on my chair on the other side of the room behind me.

14. OAKWOOD

The townhouse on Oakwood Avenue in North Bay

Dana as experienced in July 1996

I lived in an old townhouse on Oakwood Avenue in North Bay, Ontario with my daughter, Riley, who was not quite 3 years old. There were just the two of us living there at that time.

Riley in the cupboards on Oakwood Avenue

The first instance of when I noticed strange happenings in this place began one day after we came home from grocery shopping. I went to the kitchen to put the groceries away only to find all of my kitchen cabinet doors, both top and bottom, wide open. At first I thought maybe someone had broken in but then I realized that all the doors and windows were locked and nothing else was missing or out-of-place.

Dana as experienced in August 1996

Riley was about 3 years old and she had gone down for a nap so I took the opportunity to get some housework done. I was listening to some music on a CD player while I was doing the dishes.

When the CD came to an end and the music stopped I thought to myself "I thinkI will play that CD again". So I dried my hands on a tea towel and walked into the dining room where the CD player was.

As I was reaching down to press play on the machine and my finger was about 2 inches away, the CD player just all of a sudden turned itself on and started playing on its own. I hadn't touched it at all. I nearly jumped out of my skin and I ran to the phone to call my mom to tell her about it.

Dana as experienced in September 1996

In September a friend from college, Lydia, moved in with my daughter and I. It was about 4:30 pm one afternoon and Lydia and I were painting a large banner on a roll of paper on the floor of the living room for an upcoming event at the college. Lydia put some scalloped potatoes in the oven and we went about painting our sign while it cooked.

After about an hour had gone by Lydia decided to go and check on the scalloped potatoes to see if they were ready yet. But when she went into the kitchen she was surprised to see that the oven was not even turned on.

She thought that for sure she had turned the oven on but figured that she must have been mistaken. So she turned it on and we went back to doing some more painting.

After awhile we were getting really hungry so Lydia went back into the kitchen to check on dinner again. Once again the oven was turned off. There was nothing wrong with the oven; the knob had been turned to the off position. There was no one else in the house except for us.

Carsten A. as experienced in October 1996

There were multiple occasions where I would be listening to music while falling asleep on the couch and the television would just turn on by itself. The television show that would initially come on was always The Twilight Zone. Then it would keep changing channels by itself and would jump back and forth from channel 6 to channel 66.

On another occasion the power on the VCR came on by itself and it just began fast forwarding. The TV was not on so nothing was playing on the screen. It fast forwarded for a moment or two and then stopped and began going in reverse. Then it stopped again and began fast forwarding again. It did this back and forth for a minute or two before it finally just came to a complete stop and the power on the VCR went off.

When these things first started happening I just assumed that somebody outside the house had a remote or a signal was coming in the window from the neighbours across the street or something. But when I closed all the curtains and it still kept happening I knew there was just no way that could be because they worked off of an infrared signal.

Often times I would find that the elements on the stove would turn on when there was no one else in the house but me. At first I figured that I had just forgotten to turn off the stove after I had cooked something. But when I would find the elements on and I hadn't been cooking anything at all then I knew it wasn't due to forgetfulness on my part. That stove wasn't a digital stove, so the dials had to be turned to get the elements to turn on.

15. RILEY

Riley

Dana as experienced in September 1996

When Riley was 3, I was on my way out to a party one evening but decided to put her to bed for the babysitter before I left. Rather than mention the party to Riley, in case she got upset that she couldn't go to a party, I just told her that I was going to my boyfriend's house. The next morning she told me "You didn't go to your boyfriend's house, you were at a party!" When I asked the babysitter if Riley had woken up while I was out and if she had told Riley where I was going, she said that she hadn't.

Dana as experienced in June 1998

When Riley was five we were sitting at the supper-table and my boyfriend was just about to tell me something when Riley asked "Mommy, do ostrich's fly?" All of a sudden, my boyfriend asked Riley very emphatically, "Why did you ask that question?!? Why did you?!? What made you ask that?!?" He was almost yelling. I was just beginning to think that he had gone crazy so I quickly asked him "What does it matter if she asks if ostriches can fly or not?" He said "because I was just about to describe to you a chapter in the book I was reading but my mouth was full so I had to wait for a second. The chapter was about an ostrich hunt!"

16. LAKE HEIGHTS ROAD

The townhouse on Lake Heights Road in North Bay

Dana as experienced in August 2006

August 16, 2006

I spent some time cleaning up all the toys and things in Riley's room. Among the toys was a little bag of costume jewelry that I put on her book shelf for safe keeping.

August 17, 2006

Riley asks me where her bag of costume jewelry is and I told her on the book shelf. But it wasn't there. We couldn't find it anywhere. It wasn't on a shelf and it hadn't fallen off the shelf. We were leaving town for a few days to go to the Toronto Zoo so we decided that we would continue to look for it when we got back.

August 22, 2006

We come home from our trip to the zoo and Riley finds the bag of costume jewelry on the same book shelf, exactly where I had put them when I cleaned up.

Riley's stuffed lion tucked under the blankets

Dana as experienced in September 2006

September 6, 2006

Riley had just went to school on the school bus and there was no one home but me. I made Riley's bed and put Riley's pillows at the head of her bed because she had been sleeping backwards the night before and the pillows were at the foot of her bed. I put her big stuffed toy lion on the top of the covers leaning up against the pillows. An hour later I went to put the laundry away in Riley's room and the lion was tucked in under the blankets as though it were sleeping in the bed.

17. LITTLE RED SCHOOL-HOUSE

The Little Red School-House in Campbellford, Ontario

As told by Carsten R.

In 1967 my father had become too sick with a bad heart that he could no longer manage the farm. My parents sold the farm and bought a little red school-house. The school- house was built in 1912 and had doubled as a church and occasionally as a court house. There were seven unmarked graves in the backyard. My father got a job as custodian at the Campbellford District High School. Then, he took on the hobby of being a Ham Radio operator.

SAM

Sam with Carsten R. and Brenda on the concrete steps

In 1984 my father passed away. My mother later re-married. After her second husband passed away she was alone. Her neighbours Robert and Marion DeLint gave her a dog named Sam. The DeLints paid all the dog's expenses: food, veterinary bills, etc. My mother loved that little dog.

One night while my wife, Brenda, and I were staying with my mother, I woke up because a big dog had barked in the Little Red School-house. It was not Sam. He was just a little Cocker Spaniel and the sound of this bark was from a much bigger dog like a German Shepherd. My mother loved big dogs. She had big dogs in the past, all German Shepherds and all called Rex except for two in Denmark called Rossi and Freya.

Brenda had heard the bark too and asked "Did you hear the dog bark?" She got up and searched the house. There was only Sam asleep in my mother's bed room. From then on, we would once in a while be woken up by a big dog that had barked inside the school-house.

A few years later, my mother's dog, Sam, became very ill. Robert DeLint called the veterinarian to the school-house. The veterinarian consulted with Robert and my mother. They decided that it was best to have him put down. The veterinarian did it right there on the concrete steps at the entrance to the house. When Sam died, we saw his spirit come out of his body and run around on the front lawn. He seemed much younger and he was very happy.

LOCKED DOOR

Heather as experienced in 1981

The basement in the Little Red School-house has a back door, which was usually locked, that leads to the outside. Instead, the main way anyone would go to the basement was through the inside of the house using a trap door at the top of some very well weathered and worn old stairs. The trap door was always open and led into a little closet like room which had a door to the main part of the house. This main door was never closed.

Anika and I had gone down into Farmor's basement to play. When we were tired of playing down there we came up the stairs through the trap door and found that the door to the main part of the house was closed. This was very strange and unusual.

We went to open it and found that it was closed tight and would not open. We were trapped and we began to get scared. So, we started yelling and banging on the door hoping that someone would come and open it for us. But it was a nice summer day and everyone was outside and could not hear us.

We pushed and pulled with all our might but it was locked. We began to try to figure out what else to do but aside from breaking a window there really wasn't anything else we could do but wait for someone to come back inside. We waited for a couple minutes and then, getting impatient, we decided to try to rattle the door some more. This time however, the door opened very easily with just a little tug as though it had never been locked at all. We asked everyone outside if they had closed and locked the door but no one had.

THE COT IN THE BEDROOM

Dana as experienced in 2003

    I had taken my daughter, Riley, for a visit to see Farmor at the Little Red School-house in Campbellford. We always slept in the spare room at the back of the house whenever we visited. I would sleep on a big, old, antique, white, bed and Riley would sleep on an old fold up cot across the room.

    We are both late night people and had been reading into the wee hours of the morning. When we were done reading I said good night to Riley, and I turned off the little lamp with the red lampshade sitting on the night stand next to my bed. The Little Red School-house is out in the country away from all the city lights so once the lights were turned off it got very dark in the room despite there being a very large window at one end.

    It couldn't have been more than 5 minutes later when I heard Riley calling me in a very panicked voice "Mom! Mom!" I turned the little light back on and she was huddled with her back against the wall with a look of fright on her face. I asked her what was wrong and she said, "Someone grabbed my arm and wouldn't let go!"

    There was no one else in the house except for us and Farmor who was in the next room fast asleep. I asked her if she wanted to come sleep in the big white bed with me and she gratefully said "Yes!" and crawled in with me. We didn't experience anything more unusual that night but from that night on, even years later, Riley would always sleep with me in the big, white, bed and never wanted to be alone in the little cot across the room.

HAT MAN

Devin as experienced in 2009

I was looking out of the window in the basement of Farmor's house when everything went dark for a couple of seconds. It was almost like the clouds had gone across the sun. Then, the head of a faceless man came at me from the window. The man was wearing a Fedora hat. It didn't say anything or do anything. It just seemed to stare. A few moments later the head disappeared and the room went back to its normal brightness again. After I got back home I happened to read on the internet about other people who saw the same man that I saw and I discovered that he had been named the "Hat Man". I went on to read that this apparition is often known for protecting people and usually, children. I know that the Little Red School-House at one time had some unmarked graves. It was a bit creepy when I saw him but I believe that the Hat Man was just there to watch over the spirits of those who were buried on the property.

THE CHILDREN

Carsten R. as experienced in 2010

In 2010, my mother, who now was 92 years old, fell down the basement stairs and was taken to the hospital. We went down to see her. Her doctor sent her to a heart specialist and we accompanied her. The specialist said that she could no longer live alone. Therefore we stayed with her in the little red school-house.

Once in a while my mother would fall and she was becoming a little confused. She would sometimes get up during the night and fall. Sometimes, she would get up in the night and try to go down the basement stairs. The stairs were very steep and she would have fallen down if we had not been there to stop her. One time when we stopped her, we asked why she wanted to go down the stairs. She wanted to feed the horses there. Yes, she was a little confused. We put a padlock on the door to the basement.

At night my mother wanted to play Yahtzee. So, we played Yahtzee. We played Yahtzee, several times each night. There was not a single night we were there that we did not play Yahtzee. The first game was won by my mother. The next game was won by my mother. Then, the next game was won by my mother as well. She kept winning. Yahtzee is a game of chance. Skill is not involved. Therefore, using statistical probabilities, the wins should have been divided almost equally among us three players. But she would win every time.

While playing Yahtzee, we could hear children talking and giggling. They were not very loud. We could just faintly hear them occasionally. There were no children living in the area and the Little Red School-house was located in a farming community so the closest neighbours were a distance off. Brenda and I suspect that the children we heard were ghostly children and we became suspicious that these ghostly children were causing my mother to win.

SPIRITUAL ENCOUNTERS

Vera's brother, Robert

At age 92, my mother was the only one left in her family. Her parents, three sisters and two brothers had all passed away. Once in a while my mother called me by her brother's name, Robert. I would say, "I am Carsten."

"No, you are Robert" she would reply.

I slowly became aware that she really believed I was her brother Robert. Once, in the middle of the night, we heard my mother talking in her bedroom. Did she need something? Was she trying to talk to us?

I went to her bedside and sat on a chair beside her. I said, "How are you doing? Do you need anything?"

She gave me a startled look and said, "How can you be down here when you are also up there?" She pointed up. I saw nothing. But I realized that she had been talking to her brother Robert. By confusing me with Robert she saw him in two places. I could not see Robert but she could see him. However, I did see other people. One of the others was my mother's mother (Mormor). She appeared to be in her mid 20's. I got up and walked back to the second bedroom. My mother's mother followed me. There, Mormor told me that she loved me.

The next day was very eventful. My mother was determined that we should take a trip to Kingston. We spent an awful long time trying to talk her out of this trip. During our negotiations we asked her why she wanted to go to Kingston. "To meet up with my mother" was the reply. This helped our negotiations. Now we could try to convince her that her mother had never traveled to Canada and on top of that her mother had passed away quite a few years ago.

The invisible school children kept giggling and chattering quietly as my mother kept on winning at Yahtzee. My mother occasionally referred to me as Robert and we once in a while saw members of her deceased family. Her father, Niels Dam, came walking on the road in his mail man's uniform. Herman, her brother, was very recognizable. His arms had his tattoos on them. Sometimes there were many spiritual family members, sometimes only a few, and sometimes none at all.

My mother often got up in the night and would walk around and fall down. Brenda began to sleep on an easy chair in the living room to try to catch her before she would get up and fall down. Eventually my mother received a walker from her neighbours, Bob and Bill.

My cousin, Gurli, and her husband, Jens Fage-Pedersen, came from Denmark to visit my mother. Gurli is my mother's niece. The two of them sometimes went together for a walk. Brenda and I also liked to go for a walk together. One night Brenda and I went for a walk in the dark. When we reached the road and started to walk, I turned my head and looked at the schoolhouse. There was a little white cloud about the size of a pony floating off the ground by the door. The little cloud of white started to enter the schoolhouse through the door crack. I watched it disappear into the school-house.

Gurli, Carsten R., and Jens on the road that runs in front of the Little Red School-House

On another night Brenda and I walked on the road towards the nearby farms in the area. We walked about a mile and a half and then started to walk back. As we came close to the school-house we saw two people come walking from the other side of the schoolhouse, the part of the road leading to the highway. We could not make out the identity of the walkers. They appeared very dark but were obviously a man and a woman. The man and woman entered the front gate of the school-house and walked up the steps leading to the door. Then, they entered the school-house and so we thought they must be Jens and Gurli.

After we entered the school-house, we asked Jens and Gurli how they enjoyed their walk. They said, "We have not been for a walk. We have been here ever since you left for your walk."

So, the people we saw walking were not Jens and Gurli and they had apparently not been seen inside the schoolhouse. Brenda and I saw them enter the property. Where could they be?

I was sure that the two people were still on the property. Therefore I ran outside and went to look inside the garage. Nobody was in the garage. I went all around the house and garage and saw nobody. Then, I ran onto the road and looked up and down the road. I saw nobody on the road. There was nobody there.

A YELLOW CAR

Occasionally our children and their families came to the school-house for a visit on week ends. One nice sunny day we were all sitting outside on the front lawn. I saw a yellow car drive by on the road. The car had been smashed in on the side. The whole car had a huge ugly dent running almost the whole length of the car. I said, "Is it not strange that a car with that much damage would be driving on this road?"

When one of my children asked, "What? What car?" it dawned on me that nobody else had seen the yellow car.

My son-in-law, Steve, and my daughter, Heather, had been having car problems so that they could not drive their car for a while. So, the next day they borrowed our car and all of our children drove home. My mother wanted to go to town to do some banking so since we didn't have a car, one of her neighbours, Robert Delint, lent us his truck. We drove to town and my mother decided that I should do the banking for her and went to a store. Brenda also left for a different store. Then, I drove the truck to the Royal Bank.

After doing the banking I went out and got into the truck to back out of the parking space. I started the truck. I checked the back. There was nothing in the way so I started to back up. When I was far enough out that I could start to turn, I glanced in front just to make sure I would not hit any of the vehicles on my sides. Then, I hit something.

I had hit a yellow car. I was able to turn and get a little distance away from the car. I got out and what I saw was the yellow car that had driven past the school house. The car had been smashed in on the side. The whole car had a huge ugly dent running almost the whole length of the car It looked exactly as it did when it passed the school house. Now I was confused because I was wondering whether I had actually backed into it. After all, it had the damage when it drove past the school-house.

The driver of the car was terribly upset. It started to dawn on me slowly that I was the only one who had seen the yellow car drive past the school house. I had seen the car in the condition that it was now in the present and that me backing into it was indeed what had caused the smashed in side. I told this upset driver that I would pay for the repairs. My mother paid for the repairs to the yellow car.

THE HOSPITAL

Carsten R. as experienced in 2011

When my mother was about to pass away, she went to the hospital. Brenda and I sat with her in a private room. My mother told me she would see me again. I said, "I will see you later".

Then Brenda said, "We are not alone".

Sure enough, my mother's deceased family members who had been with us in the Little Red School- house were suddenly in that hospital room. Then, my mother passed away.

View of Bob and Bill Scott's farm from behind the Little Red School-House

After the funeral I wanted to be alone for a little while. I got a chair and put it behind the schoolhouse. There I sat looking up towards Bob and Bill's farm. Suddenly my mother and father appeared in front of me. They looked like they did in their mid 20's. I felt very loved. My father thanked me for coming down to the Little Red School-house to stay with my mother until she passed.

Playing UNO at the Little Red School-house

Riley as experienced in 2011

After Farmor passed away, we all gathered at her house to prepare for the memorial service and to have a BBQ in her honour. The house was full of family members and once again we had the use of the spare room at the back of the house.

We spent the evening playing UNO in the living room but there was a storm that evening and the power kept going out and coming back on so we made it an early night and retired to the bedroom. For some reason I decided to sleep in the cot at the end of the room. It was something that I hadn't done since I was young.

We settled into our beds with the door closed and the little table lamp on. We were both reading our books which we often did before bed. She eventually fell asleep with the light on. She left the light on for me because that room was making me feel nervous that night.

Then, a little while later, just as I was starting to fall asleep, my mom suddenly woke up. Half asleep and without really realizing it, she turned the light off. I was now in the complete pitch darkness of the room with the rumblings of the thunderstorm still sounding outside the house.

It wasn't more than a couple of seconds after the light was turned off that someone touched my knee for a moment before taking their hand away again.
I knew it wasn't our dog bumping into me because he was sleeping on the other side of the room and there was no one else in the room with us.

I was really scared that I was going to see someone standing there. I pulled the covers up over my head and huddled in the bed. I spent the entire night like that until about 6 or 7 in the morning when the light finally came through the window. As soon as I could I got out of the room because I didn't want to be in there anymore.

In the morning when I told grandma about what happened she said that she thought it was probably Henry's spirit (Farmor's husband who passed away many years before) trying to make me feel better.

18. STRANGE LIGHTS

CITY LIGHTS

Brenda as experienced in the 1970's

While I was living on Trout Lake, I remember looking out the window one evening and thinking to myself "Wow, I can see the city lights. They are so bright tonight." Then, I thought for a moment and realized that the direction I was facing was away from the city and towards an unpopulated, forested area. There was no city in that direction. I never did find out what the lights were.

TRAIN LIGHTS

Dana as experienced in 1989

Late one afternoon, when I was about 17, my boyfriend, Doug, and I were driving down a huge hill near my house in Chisholm. At the bottom of the hill there were fields on either side and further up was a set of train tracks that ran across the fields and the road. As we were nearing the bottom of the hill we saw a large, blue, light moving towards us to our right and we thought that a train was coming so we began to slow down.

But then as we watched we began to notice that the light began to go off the tracks and enter into the field. Worried that the train was getting into an accident we pulled over to the side of the road. Before our eyes the light began to rise up into the air to about the height of 20 feet and it sat for a few moments and hovered! That's when we realized that we didn't see any train behind this light. It was just a ball of blue light.

Doug and I both just sat in the truck, dumbfounded, for a moment. Then he said, "Let's get out of the truck and go closer!" I said, "No way! You can go but I am staying right here!"

So, he got out of the truck and started venturing closer to the glowing light in the sky. But he didn't get very far before the light quickly rose up higher into the sky and then just disappeared.

NORAD NORTH BAY UNDERGROUND COMPLEX

Dana in the summer of 1997

In 1963 Canada completed the construction of The NORAD North Bay Underground Complex which is a military air defense base situated 60 storeys beneath the surface of the Earth (NORAD stands for North American Aerospace Defense Command). The command's responsibilities are keeping watch of activities in space over North America as well as those inside Earth's atmosphere.

In 1997, I was fortunate enough to be one of the very few civilians to have a tour of the underground complex. "Due to its important, sensitive role in the security of Canada and North America, working in NORAD North Bay was limited to very few people. Over its 43-year span in air defense operations only about 17,000 Canadian and American military personnel and civilians served in the UGC." - website:www.mysteriesofcanada.com/military/norad-north-bay/
The only reason I was allowed on the tour was due to an invitation by a friend who had a friend who worked there.

The tour was quite interesting and at one point we entered a room where the "Regional Operations Control Centre/Sector Operations Control Center" computer system was situated. There was a gentleman there who was manning the control center and was telling us all about what they do there. He then asked us if we had any questions. One of the questions that came up, as a joke, was "So, do you ever have any UFOs appear on the screen?" We were prepared for some laughter and a reply of "no". To our surprise the answer was "Yes, we have". He went on to explain how many times they have had one or sometimes multiple unexplained sightings on their screens.

"The Underground Complex was put into warm storage in 2006 when we moved our NORAD operations above ground into a new facility, the Sgt David L. Pitcher Building. Tours were run for the public for a couple years after NORAD moved out, but were halted due to safety concerns. It is no longer open to the public. It's status has been in limbo ever since." - Captain Doug Newman

- 24 October 2017 in reply to questions on the website: www.mysteriesofcanada.com/military/norad-north-bay/

Dylan as experienced in the summer of 2012

It was about 5 years ago, I lived on Gladstone Street in North Bay and I was in my backyard one night with a good friend of mine, Zack. We are both smokers so we would step outside every hour or so to smoke a cigarette. It was about midnight when we noticed something very bright to the north-east of us, just floating a couple hundred feet above the underground military base.

At first, we thought it was simply a plane or a chopper, but then we realized that this object started levitating straight up. It moved up really slowly and then shot back down, very fast, in a straight line. The object continued to do this for about 5 minutes.

After that, it started to change colours. It went from a very florescent, bright, white, light to red, orange, yellow, green and blue. Sometimes, it would flash all of the colours and every once in a while it would just go out. Then, after a minute or so it would reappear.

We attempted to record what we saw and take pictures of it but we couldn't because this object would not appear properly on film. It was like taking a picture of a star with a crappy camera.

After freaking out for about a half hour we went back inside. About an hour later we went outside once again for a cigarette and to see if the object was still there. It was still there and it was still flashing all of its colours and moving about and disappearing and reappearing.

We went back inside again and when we came back an hour later and this time it was gone. I continued living at this address for another year or more and never saw anything like it again.

19. MESSAGE FROM A GENIE

Deb and Tessa

Experienced by Shelli in 2007

My mother, Deb, was diagnosed with cancer in 2006. Before she died, she was able to spend some time getting to know her twin grand daughters, Tessa and Delaney.

When the cancer worsened Deb became confined to a hospital bed and then later to a bed in her home where she eventually passed away surrounded by family in April of 2007.

A few months later my daughter, Tessa, kept telling me that she would see a genie at the end of her bed. After about a year, she told me that the genie told her "Grandma in the bed is okay". I think the "genie" was Mom, as she didn't know what a ghost or spirit was, but had just finished watching the movie Aladin.

Tessa (left) and Delaney (right)

Messages from spirits can be difficult for some to believe in. Yet, we as humans and the spirit world are closely connected. We have a desire to communicate with one another no matter where we are. Sometimes contact with spirits gives people hope and belief in maybe seeing their loved ones again. Sometimes it's a comfort to discover that we are not alone; to know that we are cared about and loved on both this side of life and on the other side.

ABOUT THE AUTHORS

Carsten R. Jorgensen and **Dana Woodard** have often worked together in the past to help each other write their own individual books. Now, for the first time, they have decided to create a father-daughter team to combine their love of writing and interest in spiritual encounters to bring you the collection that you find here.

As children and as adults they have both heard the stories their family members have told them and they wanted to share them before those stories were lost.

When Dana isn't reading or writing stories, she's probably doing her crafts, working on her family tree, or playing her video games.

When Carsten R. isn't working on his next book, he can be found playing darts, doing Tai Chi, reading, or travelling the country with his wife, Brenda, in their motor home.

OTHER TITLES BY CARSTEN R. JORGENSEN

The Saga Kings
ISBN-13: 978-0-9949338-0-5

Trying To Work For The M.N.R.
ISBN-13: 978-0-9949338-1-2

My World War Two Adventures In Denmark
ISBN-13: 978-0-9949338-2-9

One School, Two School, Old School, New School
ISBN-13: 978-0-9949338-3-6

Check out his author profile on Good Reads for any new and upcoming books that he may be working on:

www.goodreads.com/author/show/14680643.Carsten_R_Jorgensen

OTHER TITLES BY DANA WOODARD

Pond Life: Paper Quilling Projects
ISBN-13: 978-0-9938776-0-5

Don't Bug Me; I'm Quilling!: Paper Quilling Projects Vol. 2
ISBN-13: 978-0-9938776-1-2

WW2 And Other Stories From The Little Red School-House
ISBN-13: 978-0-9938776-2-9

Her author profile can be found on Good Reads at:

www.goodreads.com/author/show/9864884.Dana_Woodard

www.ingramcontent.com/pod-product-compliance
Lightning Source LLC
Chambersburg PA
CBHW071130090426
42736CB00012B/2082